Dedication Page

This book is dedicated to the women in my life.

My wife Lucy who I have been married to for 46 years and I love her more now than ever.

My two daughters Jennifer and Amanda who have turned out to be wonderful people. I am so proud of them.

My three granddaughters Corrin, Charlotte and Natalie who give us nothing but joy and smiles.

My sister Cissy, I could not have asked for a better sister and one that keeps me on my toes.

And last but not least my two son-in laws Jean Marc, Jarred and my brother-in-law George. You have earned your stripes.

My Note: God gave me a gift and kept on giving. Wow what a life.

TABLE OF CONTENT

SOMETIMES WE JUST NEED TO BE REMINDED----------------p 1

KEEP YOUR FORK--p 2

1,000 Marbles--p 5

A RUN THROUGH THE RAIN--p 8

Humor Break: HAPPY THANKSGIVING--------------------------p 11

THINK THEY WILL LET ME PLAY? -------------------------------p 12

HIS NAME IS BILL--p 15

FRIENDS---p 17

"I WANT MY COUNTRY BACK"-------------------------------------p 20

Humor Break: BOYS WILL BE BOYS-----------------------------p 23

THE CRACKED POT---p 24

THE BIG WHEEL---p 26

COFFEE? ---p 30

ATTITUDE ADJUSTMENT--p 31

Humor Break: WIFE GOING DEAF--------------------------------p 34

TABLE OF CONTENT

DADDY IS ALWAYS WITH ME------------------------------------p 35

WHAT GOES AROUND COMES AROUND----------------------p 38

ANN MRGRET--p 41

DENZEL WASHINGTON--p 43

Humor Break: WHEN HEAVEN CALLS-------------------------p 44

WORRY--p 45

MOWING THE GRASS IN IRAQ---------------------------------p 47

OUR FLAG--p 48

TAPS--p 51

MAKES YOU PROUD---p 53

USS NEW YORK--p 56

Humor Break: NOAH IN THE YEAR 2013---------------------p 57

ARE YOU JESUS---p 59

WOULD YOU RUN---p 61

Humor Break: THEY DON'T NEED GOD ANYMORE---------p 63

WHO STARTED CHRISTMAS-----------------------------------p 64

DANIEL---p 65

Humor Break: LIPSTICK--------------------------------------p 70

TRAGEDY OR BLESSING? --------------------------------------p 71

TABLE OF CONTENT

ALL THE TIME IN THE WORLD--p 73

GOT TO LOVE THIS JUDGE---p 74

CHILDREN---p 75

Humor Break: A CUP OF TEA--p 76

INSPIRATIONAL SLOGANS---p 77

Your last Humor Break: THE SHOE BOX--------------------------------p 79

INSPIRATION IS AN AWESOME THING

Inspiration is an awesome thing, it can lift you up, challenge you to do things against all odds, and help you to achieve what you and others might have thought was impossible. In all the Rocky movies that were made Rocky Balboa was inspired to overcome the many obstacles that confronted him. I always get a lump in my throat when I watch these movies because I can relate to theme on some level.

I identified with Rocky in my own life when I wrestled in high school, played football in the Army and at college. When I became a teacher and coach I was inspired by so many people and their personal stories of how they overcame obstacles and adversity in order to reach their goals.

I was influenced by my parents and mentors who encouraged me to do my best and succeed. They reminded me of phrases such as: "No Pain No Gain", "Discipline yourself so that others won't have to.", "If you are not out practicing – someone is out practicing you!" This pushed me to excel, pursue my goals, and not give up.

I have put together a collection of inspirational stories. The Authors are unknown, they created the story for a reason so let each story touch and inspire you. Totally enjoy whatever feeling that comes over you.

My Note: Inspiration is given to us by God. It is his way to keep us connected to ourselves, others, and to him, pass it on.

SOMETIMES WE JUST NEED TO BE REMINDED!

A well-known speaker started off his seminar by holding up a $20.00 bill. In the room of 200, he asked, "Who would like this $20 bill?" Hands started going up. He said, "I am going to give this $20 to one of you but first, let me do this". He proceeded to crumple up the $20 dollar bill. He then asked, "Who still wants it?" Still the hands were up in the air. Well, he replied, "What if I do this?" And he dropped it on the ground and started to grind it into the floor with his shoe. He picked it up, now crumpled and dirty. "Now, who still wants it?" Still the hands went into the air. My friends, we have all learned a very valuable lesson. No matter what I did to the money, you still wanted it because it did not decrease in value. It was still worth $20.

Many times in our lives, we are dropped, crumpled, and ground into the dirt by the decisions we make and the circumstances that come our way. We feel as though we are worthless. But no matter what has happened or what will happen, you will never lose your value. Dirty or clean, crumpled or finely creased, you are still priceless to those who DO LOVE you.

My Note: The worth of our lives comes not in what we do or who we know, but by "WHO WE ARE". You are special. Don't ever forget it."

KEEP YOUR FORK

There was a young woman who had been diagnosed with a terminal illness and had been given three months to live. So as she was getting her things in order, she contacted her pastor and had him come to her house to discuss certain aspects of her final wishes. She told him which songs she wanted sung at the service, what scriptures she would like read, and what outfit she wanted to be buried in.

Everything was in order and the pastor was preparing to leave when the young woman suddenly remembered something very important to her. "There's one more thing," she said excitedly. "What's that?" said the pastor's reply. "This is very important," the young woman continued. "I want to be buried with a fork in my right hand." The pastor stood looking at the young woman, not knowing quite what to say. "That surprises you, doesn't it?" the young woman asked. "Well, to be honest, I'm puzzled by the request," said the pastor. The young woman explained. "My grandmother once told me this story, and from there on out, I have always done so. I have also always tried to pass along its message to those I love and those who are in need of encouragement.

In all my years of attending church socials and potluck dinners, I always remember that when the dishes of the main course were being cleared, someone would inevitably lean over and say, "Keep your fork." It was my favorite part because I knew that something better was coming...like velvety chocolate cake or deep-dish apple pie. "Something wonderful, and with substance!" So, I just want people to see me there in that casket with a fork in my hand, and I want them to wonder "What's with the fork?" Then I want you to tell them: "Keep your fork the best is yet to come."

The pastor's eyes welled up with tears of joy as he hugged the young woman good-bye. He knew this would be one of the last times he would see her before her death. But he also knew that the young woman had a better grasp of heaven than he did. She had a better grasp of what heaven would be like than many people twice her age, with twice as much experience and knowledge. She knew that something better was coming.

At the funeral people were walking by the young woman's casket and they saw the pretty dress she was wearing and the fork placed in her right hand. Over and over, the pastor heard the question "What's with the fork?" And over and over he smiled. During his message, the pastor told the people of the conversation he had with the young woman shortly before she died. He also told them about the fork and about what it symbolized to her. The pastor told the people how he could not stop thinking about the fork and told them that they probably would not be able to stop thinking about it either. He was right.

So the next time you reach down for your fork, let it remind you ever so gently, that the best is yet to come. Friends are a very rare jewel, indeed. They make you smile and encourage you to succeed. They lend an ear, they share a word of praise, and they always want to open their hearts to us. Show your friends how much you care. Remember to always be there for them, even when you need them more. For you never know when it may be their time "Keep your fork." Cherish the time you have, and the memories you share. Being friends with someone is not an opportunity but a sweet responsibility.

My Note: I think of the fork every Thanksgiving, Christmas and Easter. I have a wonderful chill that comes over me for a few seconds seeing my family and we all have forks in our hands.

1000 MARBLES

The older I get, the more I enjoy Saturday mornings. Perhaps it's the quiet solitude that comes with being the first to rise, or maybe it's the unbounded joy of not having to be at work. Either way, the first few hours of a Saturday morning are most enjoyable.

A few weeks ago, I was shuffling toward the basement with a steaming cup of coffee in one hand and the morning paper in the other. What began as a typical Saturday morning, turned into one of those lessons that life seems to hand you from time to time. Let me tell you about it.

I turned the dial up into the phone portion of the band on my ham radio in order to listen to a Saturday morning swap net. Along the way, I came across an older sounding chap, with a tremendous signal and a golden voice. You know the kind; he sounded like he should be in the broadcasting business. He was telling whomever he was talking with something about "a thousand marbles." I was intrigued and stopped to listen to what he had to say.

Well, Tom, it sure sounds like you're busy with your job. I'm sure they pay you well but it's a shame you have to be away from home and your family so much. Hard to believe a young fellow should have to work sixty or seventy hours a week to make ends meet. Too bad you missed your daughter's dance recital. He continued, "Let me tell you something Tom, something that has helped me keep a good perspective on my own priorities."

And that's when he began to explain his theory of a "thousand marbles." "You see, I sat down one day and did a little arithmetic. The average person lives about seventy-five years. I know, some live more and some live less, but on average, folks live about seventy-five years. Now then, I multiplied 75 times 52 and I came up with 3,900, which is the number of Saturdays that the average person has in their entire lifetime." "Now, stick with me, Tom; I'm getting to the important part." "It took me until I was fifty-five years old to think about all this in any detail"; he went on, "and by that time I had lived through over twenty-eight hundred Saturdays. I got to thinking that if I lived to be seventy-five, I only had about a thousand of them left to enjoy."

"So I went to a toy store and bought every single marble they had. I ended up having to visit three toy stores to round up 1000 marbles. I took them home and put them inside a large, clear plastic container. Every Saturday since then, I have taken one marble out and thrown it away." "I found that by watching the marbles diminish, I focus more on the really important things in life. There is nothing like watching your time here on this earth run out to help get your priorities straight." Now let me tell you one last thing before I sign-off with you and take my lovely wife out for breakfast. This morning, I took the very last marble out of the container. I figure that if I make it until next Saturday then I have been given a little extra time. And the one thing we can all use is a little more time. "It was nice to meet you Tom, I hope you spend more time with your family, and I hope to meet you again here on the band. 75 year Old Man, this is K9NZQ, clear and going QRT, good morning!"

You could have heard a pin drop on the band when this fellow signed off. I guess he gave us all a lot to think about. I had planned to work on the antenna that morning, and then I was going to meet up with a few hams to work on the next club newsletter. Instead, I went upstairs and woke my wife up with a kiss. "Come on honey, I'm taking you and the kids to breakfast." "What brought this on?" she asked with a smile. "Oh, nothing special, it's just been a long time since we spent a Saturday together with the kids." Hey, can we stop at a toy store while we're out? I need to buy some marbles.

<u>**My Note**</u>: This story reminds me of something Winnie the Pooh said. "If you live to be a hundred, I want to live to be a hundred minus one day, so I never have to live without you."

A RUN THROUGH THE RAIN

She had been shopping with her Mom in Wal-Mart. She must have been 5 years old, this beautiful red haired, freckle-faced image of innocence. It was pouring outside. The kind of rain that gushes over the tops of rain gutters, so much in a hurry to hit the Earth it has no time to flow down the spout. Drains in the nearby parking lot were filled to capacity and some were blocked so that huge puddles laced around parked cars. We all stood there under the awning and just inside the door of the Wal-Mart. We waited, some patiently, others irritated because nature messed up their hurried day.

I am always mesmerized by rain fall. I get lost in the sound and sight of the heavens washing away the dirt and dust of the world. Memories of running, splashing as carefree as a child came pouring in as a welcome reprieve from the worries of my day. Her voice was so sweet as it broke the hypnotic trance we were all caught in. "Mom, let's run through the rain," she said. "What?" Mom asked. "Let's run through the rain!" she repeated. "No, honey. We'll wait until it slows down a bit," Mom replied. This young child waited about another minute and repeated "Mom, Let's run through the rain." "We'll get soaked if we do," Mom said. "No, we won't, Mom. That's not what you said this morning," the young girl said as she tugged at her Mom's arm. "This morning"? When did I say we could run through the rain and not get wet?" "Don't you remember?

When you were talking to Daddy about his cancer, you said, "If God can get us through this, He can get us through anything!" The entire crowd stopped dead silent. I swear you couldn't hear anything but the rain. We all stood silently. No one came or left in the next few minutes. Mom paused and thought for a moment about what she would say. Now some would laugh it off or scold her for being silly. Some might even ignore what was said. But this was a moment of affirmation in a young child's life. A time when innocent trust can be nurtured so that it will bloom into faith. "Honey, you are absolutely right. Let's run through the rain. If God lets us get wet, well maybe we just needed washing," Mom said. Then off they ran.

We all stood watching, smiling and laughing as they darted past the cars and through the puddles.

They held their shopping bags over their heads just in case. They got soaked. But they were followed by a few who screamed and laughed like children all the way to their cars. I want to believe that somewhere down the road in life; Mom will find herself reflecting back on moments they spent together, captured like pictures in the scrapbook of her cherished memories. Maybe when she watches proudly as her daughter graduates. Or as her Daddy walks her down the aisle on her wedding day. She will laugh again. Her heart will beat a little faster. Her smile will tell the world they love each other. But only they will share that precious moment when they ran through the rain believing that God would get them through. And yes, I did run. I got wet. I needed washing. Circumstances or people can take away your material possessions, they can take away your money, and they can take away your health. But no one can ever take away your precious memories…

So, don't forget to make time and take the opportunities to make memories every day!

My Note: So please take the time to run through the rain and make some memories.

Humor Break: HAPPY THANKSGIVING

A young man named John received a parrot as a gift. The parrot had a bad attitude and an even worse vocabulary. Every word out of the bird's mouth was rude, obnoxious, and laced with profanity.

John tried and tried to change the bird's attitude by consistently saying only polite words, playing soft music and anything else he could think of to "clean up" the bird's vocabulary. Finally, John was fed up and he yelled at the parrot. The parrot yelled back. John shook the parrot and the parrot got angrier and even ruder. In desperation, John threw up his hands, grabbed the bird and put him in the freezer. For a few minutes the parrot squawked and kicked and screamed. Then suddenly there was total quiet. Not a peep was heard for over a minute. Fearing that he'd hurt the parrot, John quickly opened the door to the freezer. The parrot calmly stepped out onto John's outstretched arms and said, "I believe I may have offended you with my rude language and actions. I'm sincerely remorseful for my inappropriate transgressions and I fully intend to do everything I can to correct my rude and unforgivable behavior."

John was stunned at the change in the bird's attitude. He was about to ask the parrot what had made such a dramatic change in his behavior, when the bird continued, "May I ask what the turkey did?"

THINK THEY WILL LET ME PLAY?

At a fund raising dinner for a school that serves learning disabled children, the father of one of the students delivered a speech that would never be forgotten by all who attended. After extolling the school and its dedicated staff, he offered a question. When not interfered with by outside influences, everything nature does is done with perfection. Yet my son, Shay, cannot learn things as other children do. He cannot understand things as other children do. Where is the natural order of things in my son? The audience was stilled by the query. The father continued. I believe, that when a child like Shay comes into the world, an opportunity to realize true human nature presents itself, and it comes, in the way other people treat that child.

Then he told the following story: Shay and his father had walked past a park where some boys Shay knew were playing baseball. Shay asked, "Do you think they'll let me play?" Shay's father knew that most of the boys would not want someone like Shay on their team, but the father also understood that if his son were allowed to play, it would give him a much-needed sense of belonging. Shay's father approached one of the boys on the field and asked if Shay could play. The boy looked around for guidance and, getting none, he took matters into his own hands and said, "We're losing by six runs and the game is in the eighth inning. I guess he can be on our team and we'll try to put him in to bat in the ninth inning."

In the bottom of the eighth inning, Shay's team scored a few runs but was still behind by three. In the top of the ninth inning, Shay, put on a glove and played in the outfield. Even though no hits came his way, he was obviously ecstatic just to be in the game and on the field, grinning from ear to ear as his father waved to him from the stands. In the bottom of the ninth inning, Shay's team scored again. Now, with two outs and the bases loaded, the potential winning run was on base and Shay was scheduled to be next at bat. I thought at this juncture, let Shay bat and give away their chance to win the game? Surprisingly, Shay was given the bat. Everyone knew that a hit was all but impossible because Shay didn't even know how to hold the bat properly, much less connect with the ball.

 However, as Shay stepped up to the plate, the pitcher moved in a few steps to lob the ball in softly so Shay would at least be able to make contact. The first pitch came and Shay swung clumsily and missed. The pitcher again took a few steps forward to toss the ball softly towards Shay. As the pitch came in, Shay swung at the ball and hit a slow ground ball right back to the pitcher. The pitcher picked up the soft grounder and could have easily thrown the ball to the first baseman. Shay would have been out and that would have been the end of the game. Instead, the pitcher took the ball and turned and threw the ball on a high arc to right field, far beyond the reach of the first baseman. Everyone started yelling, Shay, run to first! Run to first! Never in his life had Shay ever made it to first base. He scampered down the baseline, wide-eyed and startled. Everyone yelled, Run to second, run to second! By the time Shay rounded first base, the right fielder had the ball.

He could have thrown the ball to the second-baseman for the tag, but he understood the pitcher's intentions and intentionally threw the ball high and far over the third-baseman's head. Shay ran toward second base as the runners ahead of him deliriously circled the bases toward home. Shay reached second base, the opposing shortstop ran to him, turned him in the direction of third base, and shouted, run to third! As Shay rounded third, the boy's from both teams were screaming, Shay, Run Home! Shay ran to home, stepped on the plate, and was cheered as the hero who hit the grand slam and won the game for his team.

That day, said the father softly with tears now rolling down his face, the boys from both teams helped bring a piece of true love and humanity into this world.

My Note: Have you ever been a part of something like this? Why not?

HIS NAME IS BILL

His name is Bill. He has wild hair, wears a T-shirt with holes in it, jeans and no shoes. This was literally his wardrobe for his entire four years of college. He is kind of esoteric and very, very bright. He became a Christian while attending college. Across the street from the campus is a well-dressed, very conservative church. They want to develop a ministry to the students, but are not sure how to go about it. One day Bill decides to go there. He walks in with no shoes, jeans, his T-shirt, and wild hair. The service has already started and so Bill starts down the aisle looking for a seat. The church is completely packed and he can't find a seat. By now, people are really looking a bit uncomfortable, but no one says anything. Bill gets closer and closer and closer to the pulpit, and when he realizes there are no seats, he just squats down right on the carpet. (Although perfectly acceptable behavior at a college fellowship, trust me, this had never happened in this church before!)

By now the people are really uptight, and the tension in the air is thick. About this time, the minister realizes that from way at the back of the church, a deacon is slowly making his way toward Bill. Now the deacon is in his eighties, has silver-gray hair, and a three-piece suit. He walks with a cane and, as he starts walking toward this boy, everyone is saying to themselves that you can't blame him for what he's going to do. How can you expect a man of his age and of his background to understand some college kid on the floor? It takes a long time for the man to reach the boy.

The church is utterly silent except for the clicking of the man's cane. All eyes are focused on him. You can't even hear anyone breathing. The minister can't even preach the sermon until the deacon does what he has to do. And now they see this elderly man drop his cane on the floor. With great difficulty, he lowers himself and sits down next to Bill and worships with him so he won't be alone. Everyone chokes up with emotion. When the minister gains control, he says, "What I'm about to preach, you will never remember. What you have just seen, you will never forget."

My Note: Be careful how you live. You may be the only Bible some people will ever read.

FRIENDS

One day, when I was a freshman in high school, I saw a kid from my class walking home from school. His name was Kyle. It looked like he was carrying all of his books. I thought to myself, "Why would anyone bring home all his books on a Friday? He must really be a nerd." I had quite a weekend planned (parties and a football game with my friend's tomorrow afternoon), so I shrugged my shoulder and went on.

As I was walking, I saw a bunch of kids running toward him. They ran at him, knocking all his books out of his arms and tripping him so he landed in the dirt. His glasses went flying, and I saw them land in the grass about ten feet from him. He looked up and I saw this terrible sadness in his eyes.

My heart went out to him. So, I jogged over to him and as he crawled around looking for his glasses, I saw tears in his eyes. As I handed him his glasses, I said, "Those guys are jerks. They really should get lives." He looked at me and said, "Hey thanks!" There was a big smile on his face. It was one of those smiles that showed real gratitude.

I helped him pick up his books, and asked him where he lived. As it turned out, he lived near me, so I asked him why I had never seen him before. He said he had gone to a private school before now.

I would never hang out with a private school kid before. But we talked all the way home, and I carried some of his books. He turned out to be a pretty cool kid. I asked him if he wanted to play a little football with my friends on Saturday.

He said yes. We hung out all weekend and the more I got to know Kyle, the more I liked him, and my friends thought the same of him. Monday morning came, and there was Kyle with the huge stack of books again. I stopped him and said, "Boy, you are going to really build some serious muscles with this pile of books every day!" He just laughed and handed me half the books.

Over the next four years, Kyle and I became best friends. When we were seniors, we began to think about college. Kyle decided on Georgetown, and I was going to Duke. I knew that we would always be friends, that the miles would never be a problem. He was going to be a doctor, and I was going for business on a football scholarship.

Kyle was valedictorian of our class. I teased him all the time about being a nerd. He had to prepare a speech for graduation.

I was so glad it wasn't me having to get up there and speak. Graduation day, I saw Kyle. He looked great. He was one of those guys that really found himself during high school. He filled out and actually looked good in glasses. He had more dates than I had and all the girls loved him. Boy, sometimes I was jealous.

Today was one of those days. I could see that he was nervous about his speech. So, I smacked him on the back and said, "Hey, big guy, you'll be great!" He looked at me with one of those looks (the really grateful one) and smiled. "Thanks," he said.

As he started his speech, he cleared his throat, and began. "Graduation is a time to thank those who helped you make it through those tough years. Your parents, your teachers, your siblings, maybe a coach... but mostly your friends. I am here to tell all of you that being a friend to someone is the best gift you can give them. I am going to tell you a story."

I just looked at my friend with disbelief as he told the story of the first day we met. He had planned to kill himself over the weekend. He talked of how he had cleaned out his locker so his Mom wouldn't have to do it later and was carrying his stuff home

He looked hard at me and gave me a little smile. "Thankfully, I was saved. My friend saved me from doing the unspeakable."

I heard a gasp go through the crowd as this handsome, popular boy told us all about his weakest moment.

I saw his Mom and Dad looking at me and smiling that same grateful smile. Not until that moment did I realize its depth.

Never underestimate the power of your actions. With one small gesture you can change a person's life, for better or worse.

My Note: It is an old saying but needs to be repeated. "Do *to others as you would have them do to you" (Luke 6:31).*

I WANT MY COUNTRY BACK

I don't mean to go off on a rant here, but here's the bottom line**, I want my country back**. I want my kids to be able to walk to the store or walk to school without being abducted by some 3-time convicted child molester. And the politically correct powers that be in this country just can't seem to get over themselves with "CAN"T WE JUST HELP THIS PERSON!" No! You can't. But they're let loose to prey on more children. I want my kids back. **I want my country back**.

 I don't agree with everything this president does. I've never agreed with anything 100% that any president has done or said. You know, I was very young during the Vietnam War. So I probably missed that thing by a hair. I don't know whether I would have agreed with that or not at the time. I was too stupid to have an opinion at that point and time even though I thought I did. **I want my country back**.

  I want some semblance of respect for authority, whether I agree with it all or not. I want the Boy Scouts to be "boy" scouts, not boy and "we think she's a girl" scouts. I want Girl Scouts to be "Girl" scouts not Girl Scouts and "Bruce." **I want my country back**.

I want to be able to wake up in the morning knowing that I can walk outside without some gang-banger on parole taking my life.

I want to be able to go down and purchase a car without having to worry about 90% of the parts being made overseas in some sweatshop.

 I want my politicians, when they finally do get my vote, to do what they said they were going to do in the first place.

 I want the dishonest politicians of the world to be labeled what they are, nothing more than organized crime in a better suit.

I want people to say something and when they say something look at me in the eye. And mean what they say. Not say what they think I want to hear. And then do what they want to later politically or any other way.

I want to be able to go out and work and make a decent wage and buy a home. Half the people that are listening to me right now can't even afford to buy a house unless they're working three jobs.

And I want America to be America. All of those opportunities, all of those things that made her great, I want those returned to the forefront. If you want to come to this country we welcome you with open arms. We simply ask that you abide by our laws. I don't want you to snub your nose at our laws, and then take advantage of our opportunities, and then cling to the constitution most of which you can't even read because you don't speak the language.

I want us to secure our borders because the country is worth securing. The people that live here are worth protecting. **I want my country back**.

I want my children back. I want some semblance of what this country used to be. It's worth protecting. It's worth defending. I don't recognize this country anymore. Not politically, not philosophically, not spiritually.

Whether you like it or whether you don't. God was a part of building this great nation. To remove him is to take away the very foundation of what this country was all about. I don't care about your political correctness! I don't want to know your sexual preference! I could care less about all of that. Stop making it the headline of the day! That's not America. **I want my country back**!

And the only way I'm ever going to be able to get this country back is if I reach out to the brothers and the sisters that all feel the same way and we say "Hell No! You can't have our country." It's not for sale! So take the price tag off this country! Take the price tag off the heads of our children! Stop it already!

The politically-correct-psychobabble-hug-a-tree-experts--You are not qualified to release sex offenders back into our neighborhoods. The southern border, more than any other border, needs to be secured tomorrow. For all those that wish to come to this country to take advantage of her opportunity, to live under a constitution--a living document that breathes in and out just like you do-this country is not for sale. I should know. I'm one of the owners. You can't sell it without my permission. **I want my country back!**

By Rick Roberts – 760 KFMB Am

(Sometime around July 05, 2006)

My Note: This touched a nerve in me. I want **My Country Back** also, how about you?

Humor Break: BOYS WILL BE BOYS

A couple had two little boys ages 8 and 10, who were excessively mischievous. They were always getting into trouble and their parents knew that if any mischief occurred in their neighborhood, their sons were probably involved.

The boys' mother heard that a clergyman in town had been successful in disciplining children, so she asked if he would speak with her boys. The clergyman agreed but asked to see them individually. So the mother sent her 8 year old first, in the morning, with the older boy to see the clergyman in the afternoon.

The clergyman, a huge man with a booming voice, sat the younger boy down and asked him sternly, "Where is god?" The boys' mouth dropped open, but he made no response, sitting there with his mouth hanging open, wide-eyed. So the clergyman repeated the question in an even sterner tone, "Where is God!!?"

Again the boy made no attempt to answer. So the clergyman raised his voice even more and shook his finger in the boy's face and bellowed, "WHERE IS GOD!?" The boy screamed and bolted from the room, ran directly home and dove into his closet, slamming the door behind him. When his older brother found him in the closet, he asked, "What happened?" The younger brother, gasping for breath, replied, "We are in big trouble this time, dude. God is missing and they think we did it!"

THE CRACKED POT

A water bearer in India had two large pots, each hung on the ends of a pole that he carried across his neck. One of the pots had a crack in it, while the other pot was perfect and always delivered a full portion of water. At the end of the long walk from the stream to the house, the cracked pot arrived only half full. For a full two years this went on daily, with the bearer delivering only one and a half pots full of water to his house. Of course, the perfect pot was proud of its accomplishments, perfect for which it was made. But the poor cracked pot was ashamed of its own imperfections, and miserable that it was able to accomplish only half of what it had been made to do.

After two years of what it perceived to be a bitter failure, it spoke to the water bearer one day by the stream. "I am ashamed, and I want to apologize to you. I have been able to deliver only half my load because this crack in my side causes water to leak out all the way back to your house. Because of my flaws, you have to do all of this work, and you don't get full value from your efforts," the pot said. The bearer said to the pot, "Did you notice that there were flowers only on your side of the path, but not on the other pot's side? That's because I have always known about your flaw, and I planted flower seeds on your side of the path, and every day while we walk back, you've watered them. For two years I have been able to pick these beautiful flowers to decorate the table. Without you being just the way you are, there would not be this beauty to grace the house."

My Note: Each of us has our own unique flaws. We're all cracked pots, but it's the cracks and flaws we each have that make our lives together so very interesting and rewarding. You've just got to take each person for what they are and look for the good in them. Blessed are the flexible, for they shall not be bent out of shape. Remember to appreciate all the different people in your life!

THE BIG WHEEL

In September 1960, I woke up one morning with six hungry babies and just 75 cents in my pocket. Their father was gone. The boys ranged from three months to seven years; their sister was two. Their Dad had never been much more than a presence they feared. Whenever they heard his tires crunch on the gravel driveway they would scramble to hide under their beds. He did manage to leave $15 a week to buy groceries. Now that he had decided to leave, there would be no more beatings, but no food either.

If there was a welfare system in effect in southern Indiana at that time, I certainly knew nothing about it. I scrubbed the kids until they looked brand new and then put on my best homemade dress. I loaded them into the rusty old 51 Chevy and drove off to find a job. The seven of us went to every factory, store and restaurant in our small town. No luck. The kids stayed crammed into the car and tried to be quiet while I tried to convince whoever would listen that I was willing to learn or do anything. I had to have a job. Still no luck.

The last place we went to, just a few miles out of town was an old Root Beer Barrel drive-in that had been converted to a truck stop. It was called the Big Wheel.

An old lady named Granny owned the place and she peeked out of the window from time to time at all those kids. She needed someone on the graveyard shift, 11 at night until seven in the morning. She paid 65 cents an hour and I could start that night. I raced home and called the teenager down the street that baby-sat for people. I bargained with her to come and sleep on my sofa for a dollar a night. She could arrive with her pajamas on and the kids would already be asleep. This seemed like a good arrangement to her, so we made a deal. That night when the little ones and I knelt to say our prayers we all thanked God for finding Mommy a job.

And so I started at the Big wheel. When I got home in the morning I woke the baby-sitter up and sent her home with one dollar of my tip money-fully half of what I averaged every night. As the weeks went by, heating bills added a strain to my meager wage. The tires on the old Chevy had the consistency of penny balloons and began to leak. I had to fill them with air on the way to work and again every morning before I could go home.

One bleak fall morning, I dragged myself to the car to go home and found four tires in the back seat. New tires! There was no note, no nothing, and just those beautiful brand new tires. Had angels taken up residence in Indiana? I wondered. I made a deal with the owner of the local service station. In exchange for his mounting the new tires, I would clean up his office. I remember it took me a lot longer to scrub his floor than it did for him to do the tires.

I was now working six nights instead of five and it still wasn't enough.

Christmas was coming and I knew there would be no money for toys for the kids. I found a can of red paint and started repairing and painting some old toys lying around the house. Then I hid them in the basement so there would be something for Santa to deliver on Christmas morning.

Clothes were a worry too. I was sewing patches on top of patches on the boy's pants and soon they would be too far gone to repair. On Christmas Eve the usual customers were drinking coffee in the Big wheel. These were the truckers, Les, Frank, and Jim, and a state trooper named Joe. A few musicians were hanging around after a gig at the Legion and were dropping nickels in the pinball machine. The regulars all just sat around and talked through the wee hours of the morning and then left to get home before the sun came up.

When it was time for me to go home at seven o'clock on Christmas morning I hurried to the car. I was hoping the kids wouldn't wake up before I managed to get home and get the presents from the basement and place them under the tree. (We had cut down a small cedar tree by the side of the road down by the dump.) It was still dark and I couldn't see much, but there appeared to be some dark shadows in the car-or was that just a trick of the night? Something certainly looked different, but it was hard to tell what.

When I reached the car I peered warily into one of the side windows. Then my jaw dropped in amazement. My old battered Chevy was filled full to the top with boxes of all shapes and sizes. I quickly opened the driver's side door, scrabbled inside and kneeled in the front facing the back seat.

Reaching back, I pulled off the lid of the top box. Inside was whole case of little blue jeans, sizes 2-10! I looked inside another box; it was full of shirts to go with the jeans. Then I peeked inside some of the other boxes. *There was candy and nuts and bananas and bags of groceries.* There was an enormous ham for baking, and canned vegetables and potatoes. There was pudding and Jell-O and cookies, pie filling and flour. There was a whole bag of laundry supplies and cleaning items. And there were five toy trucks and one beautiful little doll.

Yes, there were angels in Indiana that long-ago December. And they all hung out at the Big Wheel Truck Stop.

MY Note: I hope this story has touched your heart as it has touched mine. Let's keep the BIG WHEEL ROLLING.

COFFEE?

A group of alumni, highly established in their careers, got together to visit their old university professor. The conversation soon turned into complaints about stress in work and life.

Offering his guest coffee, the professor went to the kitchen and returned with a large pot of coffee and an assortment of cups – porcelain, plastic, glass, crystal, some plain-looking, some expensive, and some exquisite – telling them to help themselves to the coffee.

After all the students had a cup of coffee in hand, the professor said:

"If you noticed, all the nice looking expensive cups were taken up, leaving behind the plain and cheap ones. While it is but normal for you to want only the best for yourselves, that is the source of your problems and stress.

Be assured that the cup itself adds no quality to the coffee. In most cases, it's just more expensive and in some cases even hides what we drink. What all of you really wanted was coffee, not the cup, but you consciously went for the best cups and then began eyeing each other's cups.

Now consider this: Life is the coffee, and the jobs, money and position in society are the cups. They are just tools to hold and contain life, and the type of cup we have does not define nor change the quality of life we live. Sometimes, by concentrating only on the cup, we fail to enjoy the coffee God has provided us."

<u>MY Note</u>: God brews the coffee, not the cups…So enjoy the coffee.

ATTITUDE ADJUSTMENT

I sat in my seat of the Boeing 767 waiting for everyone to hurry and stow their carry-ons and grab a seat so we could start what I was sure to be a long, uneventful flight home.

With the huge capacity and slow moving people taking their time to stuff luggage far too big for the overhead and never paying much attention to holding up the growing line behind them, I simply shook my head knowing that this flight was not starting out very well. I was anxious to get home to see my loved ones so I was focused on my issues and just felt like standing up and yelling for some of these clowns to get their act together. I knew I couldn't say a word so I just thumbed thru the "Sky Mall" magazine from the seat pocket in front of me.

With everyone finally seated, we just sat there with the cabin door open and no one in any hurry to get us going although we were well past the scheduled take off time.

Just then, the attendant came on the intercom to inform us all that we were being delayed. The entire plane let out a collective groan. She resumed speaking to say "We are holding the aircraft for some very special people.

Why the hoopla over these folks? I was expecting some celebrity or sport figure to be the reason for the holdup...Just get their butts in a seat and let's hit the gas I thought. The attendant came back on the speaker to announce in a loud and excited voice that we were being joined by several U.S. Military personal returning home from Iraq!!!

Just as they walked on board, the entire plane erupted into applause. The men and women were a bit taken by surprise by the 340 people cheering for them as they searched for their seats.

They were having their hands shaken and touched by almost everyone who was within an arm's distance of them as they passed down the aisle. One elderly woman kissed the hand of one of the Military personal as he passed by her. The applause whistles and cheering didn't stop for a long time.

When we were finally airborne, I was not the only civilian checking his conscience as to the delays in me getting home, finding my easy chair, a cold beverage and the remote in my hand. These men and women had done for all of us and I had been complaining silently about me and my issues I took for granted the everyday freedoms I enjoy and the conveniences of the American way of life. I took for granted that others had paid the price for my ability to moan and complain about a few minutes delay to me while those Heroes were going home to their loved ones.

I attempted to get my selfish outlook back in order and minutes before we landed, I suggested to the attendant that she announce over the speaker a request for everyone to remain in their seats until our heroes were allowed to gather their things and be first off the plane.

The cheers and applause continued until the last Military person stepped off and we all rose to go about our too often taken for granted everyday freedoms. I felt proud of them. I felt it an honor and a privilege to be among the first to welcome them home and say "Thank You for a job well done." I vowed that I will never forget that flight nor the lesson learned. I can't say it enough, thank you to those Veterans and active servicemen and women who may read this and say a prayer for those who cannot because they are no longer with us.

<u>My Note</u>: GOD BLESS AMERICA! WELCOME HOME! AND THANKS FOR A JOB WELL DONE!!!

Humor Break: WIFE GOING DEAF?

A fellow goes to the doctor, "I'm really worried about my wife. I ask her a question and she never answers, I think she's going deaf." "That's possible," answers the doctor. "But in order to help, we'll have to determine the extent of her hearing problem. I suggest that you run a little test to see how bad the problem really is."

At that point the doctor gave him instructions. The next day the two are out on the golf course. She's plum-bobbing a putt, and he steps 15 feet away from her and asks, "Which way do you think the ball will break?" No answer. He steps 5 feet closer and asks the same question, and still no answer. Again 5 feet closer and again still no answer. Finally he moves to within inches of her ear and asks, "Which way do you think the ball will break?"

She snaps, "For the fourth and final time, I think the darn thing breaks to the left!"

DADDY IS ALWAYS WITH ME

(Daddy's poem)

(If this one does not get you nothing will)

Her hair was up in a ponytail, her favorite dress tied with a bow. Today was Daddy's Day at school, and she couldn't wait to go.

But her mommy tried to tell her, that she probably should stay home. Why the kids might not understand, if she went to school alone.

But she was not afraid: She knew just what to say. What to tell her classmates of why he wasn't there today.

But still her mother worried, for her to face this day alone. And that was why once again, she tried to keep her daughter home.

But the little girl went to school, eager to tell them all, about a dad she never sees a dad who never calls.

There were daddies along the wall in back, for everyone to meet. Children squirming impatiently, anxious in their seats.

One by one as the seconds slowly passed, the teacher called a student to introduce their Dad.

At last the teacher called her name, every child turned to stare. Each of them was searching, for a man who wasn't there.

"Where's her daddy at?" she heard a boy call out. "She probably doesn't have one," another student dared to shout.

And from somewhere near the back, she heard a daddy say, "Looks like another deadbeat dad, too busy to waste his day."

The words did not offend her, as she smiled up at her Mom. And looked back at her teacher, who told her to go on.

And with hands behind her back, slowly she began to speak. And out from the mouth of a child, came words incredibly unique.

"My Daddy couldn't be here, because he lives so far away. But I know he wishes he could be, since this is such a special day."

And though you cannot meet him, I wanted you all to know all about my daddy and how much he loves me so.

He loved to tell me stories, he taught me to ride my bike. He surprised me with pink roses, and taught me to fly a kite.

We used to share fudge sundaes, and ice cream in a cone. And though you cannot see him, I'm not standing here alone.

"Cause my daddy's always with me, even though we are apart. I know because he told me, He'll forever be in my heart."

With that, her little hand reached up, and lay across her chest. Feeling her own heartbeat, beneath her favorite dress.

And from somewhere in the crowd of dads, her mother stood in tears. Proudly watching her daughter, who was wise beyond her years?

For she stood up for the love of a man not in her life. Doing what was best for her, doing what was right.

And when she dropped her hand back down, staring straight into the crowd. She finished with a voice so soft, but its message clear and loud.

"I love my daddy very much, he's my shining star." And if he could, he'd be here, but heaven's just too far.

You see he was a fireman and died just this past year. When airplanes hit the towers and taught Americans to fear.

But sometimes when I close my eyes, it's like he never went away. And then she closed her eyes, and saw him there that day.

And to her mother's amazement, she witnessed with surprise. A room full of daddies and children, all starting to close their eyes.

Who knows what they saw before them, who knows what they felt inside. Perhaps for merely a second, they saw him at her side.

"I know you're with me Daddy," to the silence she called out. And what happened next made believers, of those once filled with doubt.

Not one in the room could explain it, for each of their eyes had been closed. But there on the desk beside her, was a fragrant long-stemmed pink rose.

And a child was blessed, if only for a moment, by the love of her shining bright star. And given the gift of believing, that heaven is never too far.

My Note: They say it takes a minute to find a special person, an hour to appreciate them, a day to love them, but then an entire life to forget them.

WHAT GOES AROUND COMES AROUND

He almost didn't see the old lady, stranded on the side of the road, but even in the dim light of day, he could see she needed help. So he pulled up in front of her Mercedes and got out. His Pontiac was still sputtering when he approached her. Even with the smile on his face, she was worried. No one had stopped to help for the last hour or so. Was he going to hurt her? He didn't look safe; he looked poor and hungry.

He could see that she was frightened, standing out there in the cold. He knew how she felt. It was that chill which only fear can put in you. He said, "I'm here to help you, ma'am. Why don't you wait in the car where it's warm? By the way, my name is Bryan Anderson."

Well, all she had was a flat tire, but for an old lady, that was bad enough. Bryan crawled under the car looking for a place to put the jack, skinning his knuckles a time or two. Soon he was able to change the tire. But he had to get dirty and his hands hurt. As he was tightening up the lug nuts, she rolled down the window and began to talk to him. She told him that she was from St. Louis and was only just passing through. She couldn't thank him enough for coming to her aid.

Bryan just smiled as he closed her trunk. The lady asked how much she owed him. Any amount would have been all right with her. She already imagined all the awful things that could have happened had he not stopped. Bryan never thought twice about being paid. This was not a job to him. This was helping someone in need; and God knows there were plenty who had given him a hand in the past. He had lived his whole life that way, and it never occurred to him to act any other way.

He told her that if she really wanted to pay him back, the next time she saw someone who needed help, she could give that person the assistance they needed, and Bryan added, "And think of me." He waited until she started her car and drove off. It had been a cold and depressing day, but he felt good as he headed for home disappearing into the twilight.

A few miles down the road the lady saw a small café. She went in to grab a bite to eat and take the chill off before she made the last leg of her trip home. It was a dingy looking restaurant. Outside were two old gas pumps. The whole scene was unfamiliar to her; the waitress came over and brought a clean towel to wipe her wet hair. She had a sweet smile, one that even being on her feet for the whole day couldn't erase. The lady noticed the waitress was about eight months pregnant, but she never let the strain and aches change her attitude. The old lady wondered how someone who had so little could be so giving to a stranger. Then she remembered Bryan.

After the lady finished her meal, she paid with a hundred dollar bill. The waitress quickly went to get change for her hundred dollar bill, but the old lady had slipped right out the door. She was gone by the time the waitress came back. The waitress wondered where the lady could be. Then she noticed something written on the napkin. There were tears in her eyes when she read what the lady wrote: "You don't owe me anything. I have been there too. Somebody once helped me out, the way I'm helping you. If you really want to pay me back, here is what you do: Do not let this chain of love end with you."

Under the napkin were four more $100 bills.

Well, there were tables to clear, sugar bowls to fill, and people to serve, but the waitress made it through another day. That night when she got home from work and climbed into bed, she was thinking about the money and what the lady had written. How could the lady have known how much she and her husband needed it? With the baby due next month, it was going to be hard.

She knew how worried her husband was, and as he lay sleeping next to her, she gave him a soft kiss and whispered soft and low, "Everything's going to be all right! I love you, Bryan Anderson."

<u>**My Note**</u>: **Don't ever forget** "What goes around comes around."

ANN MARGRET

Original Message from: Katie Todd.   Date: 01/31/05

Subject: FW: Ann Margaret Viet Nam 1966.

Richard, (my husband), never really talked a lot about his time in Viet Nam other than he had been shot by a sniper. However, he had a rather grainy, 8x10 black and white photo he had taken at a USO show of Ann Margret with Bob Hope in the background that was one of his treasures.

A few years ago, Ann Margret was doing a book signing at a local bookstore. Richard wanted to see if he could get her to sign the treasured photo so he arrived at the bookstore at 12 o'clock for the 7:30 signing.

When I got there after work, the line went all the way around the bookstore, circled the parking lot and disappeared behind a parking garage. Before her appearance, bookstore employees announced that she would sign only her book and no memorabilia would be permitted.

Richard was disappointed, but wanted to show her the photo and let her know how much those shows meant to lonely GI's so far from home. Ann Margret came out looking as beautiful as ever and, as second in line, it was soon Richard's turn.

He presented the book for her signature and then took out the photo. When he did, there were many shouts from the employees that she would not sign it. Richard said, "I understand. I just wanted her to see it."

She took one look at the photo, tears welled up in her eyes and she said, "This is one of my gentlemen from Viet Nam and I most certainly will sign his photo. I know what these men did for their country and I always have time for "My gentlemen."

With that, she pulled Richard across the table and planted a big kiss on him. She then made quite a to-do about the bravery of the young men she met over the years, how much she admired them, and how much she appreciated them. There weren't too many dry eyes among those close enough to hear. She then posed for pictures and acted as if he was the only one there.

Later at dinner, Richard was very quiet. When I asked if he'd like to talk about it, my big strong husband broke down in tears. "That's the first time anyone ever thanked me for my time in the Army," he said.

That night was a turning point for him. He walked a little straighter and, for the first time in years, was proud to have been a Vet. I'll never forget Ann Margret for her graciousness and how much that small act of kindness meant to my husband.

I now make it a point to say "Thank you" to every person I come across who served in our Armed Forces. Freedom does not come cheap and I am grateful for all those who have served their country.

My Note: WOW!!!

DENZEL WASHINGTON

(The Media missed this one)

Don't know whether you heard about this but Denzel Washington and his family visited the troops at Brook Army Medical Center, in San Antonio, Texas (BAMC). This is where soldiers who have been evacuated from Germany come to be hospitalized in the United States, especially burn victims. There are some buildings there called Fisher Houses. The Fisher house is a Hotel where soldiers' families can stay, for little or no charge, while their soldier is staying in the Hospital. BAMC has quite a few of these houses on base, but as you can imagine, they are almost filled most of the time.

While Denzel Washington was visiting BAMC, they gave him a tour of one of the Fisher Houses. He asked how much one of them would cost to build. He took his check book out and wrote a check for the full amount right there on the spot. The soldiers overseas were amazed to hear this story and want to get the word out to the American public, because it warmed their hearts to hear it.

My Note: The question I have:
Is why does Alec Baldwin, Madonna, Sean Penn and other Hollywood types make front page news with their anti-everything America and Denzel Washington's Patriotism doesn't even make page 3 in the Metro section of any newspaper except the local Newspaper in San Antonio.

Humor Break: WHEN HEAVEN CALLS

An engineer dies and reports to the pearly gates. St. Peter checks his dossier and says, "Ah, you're an engineer – you're in the wrong place." So, the engineer reports to the gates of hell and is let in.

Pretty soon, the engineer gets dissatisfied with the level of comfort in hell, and starts designing and building improvements. After a while, they've got air conditioning and flush toilets and escalators, and the engineer is a pretty popular guy.

One day, God calls Satan up on the telephone and says with a sneer, "So, how's it going down there in hell?"

Satan replies, "Hey, things are going great. We've got air conditioning and flush toilets and escalators, and there's no telling what this engineer is going to come up with next."

God replies, "What??? You've got an engineer? That's a mistake – he should never have gotten down there; send him up here."

Satan says, "No way." I like having an engineer on the staff, and I'm keeping him." God says, "Send him back up here or I'll sue."

Satan laughs uproariously and answers, "Yeah, right. And just where are you going to get a lawyer?"

WORRY

Is there a magic cutoff period when offspring become accountable for their own actions? Is there a wonderful moment when parents can become detached spectators in the lives of their children and shrug, "It's their life," and feel ok?

When I was in my twenties, I stood in a hospital corridor waiting for doctors to put a few stitches in my daughters head. I asked, "When do you stop worrying?" The nurse said, "When they get out of the accident stage." My mother just smiled faintly and said nothing.

When I was in my thirties, I sat on a little chair in a classroom and heard how one of my children talked incessantly, disrupted the class, and was headed for a career making license plates. As If to read my mind, a teacher said "Don't worry, they all go through this stage and then you can sit back, relax and enjoy them." My mother just smiled faintly and said nothing.

When I was in my forties, I spent a lifetime waiting for the phone to ring, the cars to come home, the front door to open. A friend said, "They're trying to find themselves. Don't worry, in a few years, you can stop worrying. They'll be adults." My mother just smiled faintly and said nothing.

By the time I was fifty, I was sick & tired of being vulnerable. I was still worrying over my children, but there was a new wrinkle. There was nothing I could do about it. My mother just smiled faintly and said nothing. I continued to anguish over their failures, be tormented by their frustrations and absorbed in their disappointments.

My friends said that when my kids got married I could stop worrying and lead my own life. I wanted to believe that, but I was haunted by my mother's warm smile and her occasional, "You look pale. Are you all right? Call me the minute you get home. Are you depressed about something?"

Can it be that parents are sentenced to a lifetime of worry? Is concern for one another handed down like a torch to blaze the trail of human frailties and the fears of the unknown? Is concern a curse or is it a virtue that elevates us to the highest form of life?

One of my children became quite irritable recently, saying to me, "Where were you? I've been calling for three days, and no one answered. I was worried."

I smiled a warm smile. The torch has been passed.

My Note: Let's hope that torch never goes out.

MOWING THE GRASS IN IRAQ

There was a soldier stationed in Iraq, stationed in a big sand box. He asked his wife to send him dirt (U.S. soil), fertilizer and some grass seed so he could have the sweet aroma and feel the grass grow beneath his feet. When the men of the squadron have a mission they are going on they take turns walking through the grass and the American soil to bring them good luck.

The soldier even cuts the grass with a pair of scissors. Sometimes we are in such a hurry that we don't stop and think about the little things that we take for granted.

My Note: How proud they are; how proud we should be!

OUR FLAG

(Did You Know?)

Have you ever noticed how the honor guard pays meticulous attention to correctly fold the American flag 13 times? You probably thought it was to symbolize the original 13 colonies, but there is much more.

The 1st fold of our flag is a symbol of life.

The 2nd fold is a symbol of our belief in eternal life.

The 3rd fold is made in honor and remembrance of the veterans departing our ranks, who gave a portion of their lives for the defense of our country to attain peace throughout the world.

The 4th fold represents our weaker nature, for as American citizens trusting in God, it is to Him we turn in times of peace as well as in time of war, for His divine guidance.

The 5th fold is a tribute to our country, for in the words of Stephen Decatur, "Our Country, in dealing with other countries, may she always be right: but it is still our country, right or wrong.

The 6th fold is for where our hearts lie. It is with our heart that we pledge allegiance to the flag of the United States of America, and the Republic for which it stands, one Nation under god, Indivisible, with Liberty and Justice for all.

The 7th fold is a tribute to our Armed Forces, for it is through them that we protect our country and our flag against all her enemies, whether they be found within our without the boundaries of our republic.

The 8th fold is a tribute to the one who entered into the valley of the shadow of Death, that we might see the light of day.

The 9th fold is a tribute to womanhood, and Mothers. For it has been through their faith, their love, loyalty and devotion that the character of the man and women who have made this country great, has been molded.

The 10th fold is a tribute to Fathers, for they too, have given their sons and daughters for the defense of our country since they were first born.

The 11th fold represents the lower portions of the seal of King David and King Solomon and glorifies in the Hebrews eyes, the God of Abraham, Isaac and Jacob.

The 12th fold represents an emblem of eternity and glorifies in the Christians eyes, God the Father, the son and Holy Spirit.

The 13th fold, or when the flag is completely folded, the stars are uppermost, reminding us of our nation's motto, "In God We Trust".

After the flag is completely folded and tucked in, it takes on the appearance of a cocked hat, ever reminding us of the soldiers who served under General George Washington, and the Sailors and Marines who served under Captain John Paul Jones, who were followed by their comrades and shipmates in the Armed Forces of the United States, preserving for us the rights, privileges and freedoms we enjoy today.

There are some traditions and ways of doing things that have important deep meanings. In the future, when you see flags folded, now you will know why.

My Note: Our flag is not just a piece of cloth it is a symbol. One that makes me proud. How about you?

TAPS

We in the United States have all heard the haunting song, "Taps". It's the song that gives us that lump in our throats and usually tears in our eyes.

But, do you know the story behind the song? This is one story that is shared a lot. I think you will be interested to find out about its humble beginnings.

Reportedly, it all began in 1862 during the Civil War, when Union Army Captain Robert Ellicombe was with his men near Harrison's Landing in Virginia.

The Confederate Army was on the other side of the narrow strip of land. During the night, Captain Ellicombe heard the moans of a soldier who lay severely wounded on the field. Not knowing if it was a Union or Confederate soldier, the Captain decided to risk his life and bring the stricken man back for medical attention. Crawling on his stomach through the gunfire, the Captain reached the stricken soldier and began pulling him toward his encampment.

When the Captain finally reached his own lines, he discovered it was actually a Confederate soldier, but the soldier was dead. The Captain lit a lantern and suddenly caught his breath and went numb with shock. In the dim light, he saw the face of the soldier. It was his own son.

The boy had been studying music in the south when the war broke out. Without telling his father, the boy enlisted in the Confederate Army.

The following morning, heartbroken, the father asked permission of his superiors to give his son a full military burial, despite his enemy status. His request was only partially granted.

The Captain had asked if he could have a group of Army band members play a funeral dirge for his son at the funeral. The request was turned down. Since the soldier was a Confederate.

But, out of respect for the father, they did say they could give him only one musician. The Captain chose a bugler. He asked the bugler to play a series of musical notes he had found on a piece of paper in the pocked of the dead youth's uniform. The wish was granted. The haunting melody, we now know as "Taps". Now used at all military funerals.

Lyrics were added later: "Day is done…Gone the sun…From the lakes…From the hills…From the sky…All is well…Safely rest…God is nigh.

Fading light…Dims the sight and a star…Gems the sky…Gleaming bright…From afar…Drawing nigh…Falls the night.

Thanks and praise…For our days…Neath the sun…Neath the stars…Neath the sky…As we go…This we know…God is nigh.

My Note: I, too have felt the chills while listening to "Taps" but I have never seen all the words to the song until now. I didn't even know there was more than one verse. I also never knew the story behind the song. I now have an even deeper respect for the song than I ever had before.

MAKES YOU PROUD

(Tomb of the Unknown Soldier)

(If this does not touch your heart then nothing will.)

On jeopardy one night, the final question was how many steps does the guard take during his walk across the tomb of the Unknowns...All three missed it.

This is really an awesome sight to watch if you've never had the chance you should make the time.

<u>TOMB OF THE UNKNOWN SOLDIER:</u>

1. How many steps does the guard take during his walk across the tomb of the Unknowns and why? 21 steps. It alludes to the twenty-one gun salute, which is the highest honor given any military or foreign dignitary.

2. How long does he hesitate after his about face to begin his return walk and why? 21 seconds for the same reason as answer number 1.

3. Why are his gloves wet? His gloves are moistened to prevent his losing his grip on the rifle.

4. Does he carry his rifle on the same shoulder all the time and if not, why not? He carries the rifle on the shoulder away from tomb. After his march across the path, he executes an about face and moves the rifle to the outside shoulder.

5. How often are the guards changed? Guards are changed every thirty minutes, twenty-four hours a day, and 365 days a year.

6. What are the physical traits of the guard limited to? For a person to apply for guard duty at the tomb he must be between 5'10" and 6'2" tall and his waist size cannot exceed 30 inches. Other requirements of the Guard: They must commit 2 years of life to guard the tomb, live in a barracks under the tomb, and cannot drink any alcohol or smoke on or off duty for the rest of their lives. They cannot swear in public for the rest of their lives and cannot disgrace the uniform or the tomb in any way. After two years, the guard is given a wreath pin that is worn on their lapel signifying they served as guard of the tomb. There are only 400 presently worn. The guards must obey these rules for the rest of their lives or give up the wreath pin.

The shoes are specially made with very thick soles to keep the heat and cold from their feet. There are metal heel plates that extend to the top of the shoe in order to make the loud click as they come to a halt. There are no wrinkles, folds or lint on the uniform. Guards dress for duty in front of a full-length mirror.

The first six months of duty a guard cannot talk to anyone, nor watch TV. All off duty time is spent studying the 175 notable people laid to rest in Arlington National Cemetery. A guard must memorize who they are and where they are interred. Among the notables are: President Taft, Joe E. Lewis (the boxer) and Medal of Honor winner Audie Murphy, (the most decorated soldier of WWII) and of Hollywood fame.

Every guard spends five hours a day getting his uniforms ready for guard duty.

My Note: In 2003 as Hurricane Isabelle was approaching Washington, DC, our US Senate/House took 2 days off with anticipation of the storm. On the ABC evening news, it was reported that because of the dangers from the hurricane, the military members assigned the duty of guarding the Tomb of the Unknown Soldier were given permission to suspend the assignment. They respectfully declined the offer, "NO way, Sir!" Soaked to the skin, marching in the pelting rain of a tropical storm, they said that guarding the Tomb was not just an assignment; it was the highest honor that can be afforded to a serviceperson. The Tomb has been patrolled continuously, 24/7, since 1930

A Special Prayer for the Unknown Soldier:

ETERNAL REST GRANT THEM O LORD, AND LET PERPETUAL LIGHT SHINE UPON THEM.

USS NEW YORK

It was built with 24 tons of scrap steel from the World Trade Center. It is the fifth in a new class of warship – designed for missions that include special operations against terrorists. It will carry a crew of 360 sailors and 700 combat-ready Marines to be delivered ashore by helicopters and assault craft.

Steel from the World Trade Center was melted down in a foundry in Amite, LA to cast the ship's bow section. When it was poured into the molds on Sept. 9, 2003, "those big rough steelworkers treated it with total reverence." Recalled Navy Captain, Kevin Wensing, who was there. "It was a spiritual moment for everybody there."

Junior Chavers, foundry operations manager, said that when the trade center steel first arrived, he touched it with his hand and the "hair on my neck stood up." "It had a big meaning to it for all of us." He said. "They knocked us down. They can't keep us down. We're going to be back."

The ship's motto? "Never forget"

My Note: Have we forgotten**?**

Humor Break: NOAH IN THE YEAR 2013

In the year 2013, the Lord came unto Noah, who was now living in the United States, and said, "Once again, the earth has become wicked and over-populated, and I see the end of a flood before me. Build another Ark and save 2 of every living thing along with a few good humans."

He gave Noah the blueprints, saying, "You have 6 months to build the Ark before I will start the un-ending rain for 40 days and 40 nights."

Six months later, the Lord looked down and saw Noah weeping in his yard but no Ark. "Noah!" He roared, "I'm about to start the rain! Where is the Ark?"

"Forgive me, Lord, "begged Noah, "but things have changed. I needed a building permit. I've been arguing with the inspector about the need for a sprinkler system. My neighbors claim that I've violated the neighborhood zoning laws by building the Ark in my yard and exceeding the height limitations. We had to go to the development Appeal Board for a decision.

Then the Department of Transportation demanded a bond be posted for the future cost of moving power lines and other overhead obstructions, to clear the passage for the Ark's move to the sea. I told them that the sea would be coming to us, but they would hear nothing of it.

Getting the wood was another problem. There's a ban on cutting local trees in order to save the spotted owl. I tried to convince the environmentalists that I needed the wood to save the owls- but no go!

When I started gathering the animals, an animal rights group sued me. They insisted that I was confining wild animals against their will. They argued the accommodations were too restrictive, and it was cruel and inhumane to put so many animals in a confined space.

Then the EPA ruled that I couldn't build the Ark until they'd conducted an environmental impact study on your proposed flood.

I'm still trying to resolve a complaint with the Human Rights Commission on how many minorities I'm supposed to hire for my building crew. Immigration and Naturalization is checking the green-card status of most of the people who want to work.

The trades unions say I can't use my sons. They insist I have to hire only Union workers with Ark-building experience.

To make matters worse, the IRS seized all my assets, claiming I'm trying to leave the country illegally with endangered species.

So, "forgive me, Lord, but it would take at least 10 years for me to finish this Ark."

Suddenly the skies cleared, the sun began to shine, and a rainbow stretched across the sky. Noah looked up in wonder and asked, "You mean you're not going to destroy the world?"

"No," said the Lord. "The government beat me to it.

ARE YOU JESUS?

A few years ago a group of salesmen went to a regional sales convention in Chicago. They had assured their wives that they would be home in plenty of time for Friday night's dinner. In their rush through the terminal, with tickets and briefcase, one of these salesmen inadvertently kicked over a table which held a display of apples. Apples flew everywhere. Without stopping or looking back, they all managed to reach the plane in time for their nearly missed boarding. All But one!!! He paused, took a deep breath, got in touch with his feelings, and experienced a twinge of compassion for the girl whose apple stand had been overturned. He told his buddies to go on without him, waved good-bye, told one of them to call his wife when they arrived at their home destination and explain his taking a later flight. Then he returned to the terminal where the apples were all over the terminal floor. He was glad he did. The 16 year old girl was totally blind! She was softly crying, tears running down her cheeks in frustration, and at the same time helplessly groping for her spilled produce as the crowd swirled about her, no one stopping and no one to care for her plight.

The salesman knelt on the floor with her, gathered up the apples, put them back on the table and helped organize her display. As he did this, he noticed that many of them had become battered and bruised; these he set aside in another basket. When he had finished, he pulled out his wallet and said to the girl, "Here, please take this $40 for the damage we did. Are you okay? She nodded through her tears. He continued on with, "I hope we didn't spoil your day too badly."

As the salesman started to walk away, the bewildered blind girl called out to him, "Mister…" He paused and turned to look back into those blind eyes she continued, "Are you Jesus?" He stopped in mid stride, and he wondered. Then slowly he made his, way to catch the later flight with that question burning and bouncing about in his soul.

My Question: "Are you Jesus?" Do people mistake you for Jesus? That's our destiny, is it not? To be so much like Jesus that people cannot tell the difference as we live and interact with a world that is blind to his love, life, and grace. If we claim to know him, we should live, walk, and act as he would. Knowing him is more than simply quoting scripture and going to church. It's actually living the word as life unfolds day to day.

MY Note: You are the apple of his eye even though we too have been bruised by a fall. He stopped what he was doing and picked you and me up on a hill called Calvary and paid in full for our damaged fruit.

WOULD YOU RUN?

One Sunday morning during service, a 2,000 member congregation was surprised to see two men enter, both covered from head to toe in black and carrying submachine guns. One of the men proclaimed "Anyone willing to take a bullet for Christ remain where you are." Immediately, the choir fled, the deacons fled, and most of the congregation fled. Out of the 2,000 there only remained around 20.

The man who had spoken took off his hood. He then looked at the preacher and said "Okay Pastor, I got rid of all the hypocrites, now you may begin your service. Have a nice day!" And the two men turned and walked out.

Question: Would you run?

Isn't it funny?

"How simple it is for people to trash God, and then wonder why the world is in the condition it is today."

"How we believe what the newspapers say, but question what the Bible says."

"How everyone wants to go to heaven, provided they do not have to believe, think, say, or do anything the Bible says."

"How someone can say "I believe in God, but still follow Satan." Who, by the way also, believes in God.

"How you can send a thousand 'jokes' through e-mail and they spread like wildfire, but when you start sending messages regarding the Lord, you think twice about sharing."

"How the lewd, crude, vulgar and obscene pass freely through cyberspace, but the public discussion of Jesus is suppressed in the school and work place."

"How someone can be so fired up for Christ on Sunday, but be an invisible Christian the rest of the week."

"How when you go to forward a message about God on your computer, you will not send it to many on your address list because you're not sure what they believe."

"How you can be more worried about what other people think of you, than what god thinks of you."

***MY Note*:** A prayer for you:

May the Lord bless you and keep you.

May the Lord make his face to shine upon you, and be gracious to you.

May the Lord lift up his favor upon you and give you his peace (Numbers6:22-27).

Humor Break: THEY DON'T NEED GOD ANYMORE

One day a group of scientists got together and decided that man had come a long way and no longer needed God. So they picked one scientist to go and tell him that they were done with him.

The scientist walked up to God and said, "God, we've decided that we no longer need you. We're to the point that we can clone people and do many miraculous things, so why don't you just go on and get lost."

God listened very patiently and kindly to the man and after the scientist was done talking, God said: "Very well, how about this, let's have a man making contest." To which the scientist replied, "Okay, great!"

But God added, "Now, we're going to do this just like I did back in the old days with Adam." The scientist said, "Sure, no problem," and bent down and grabbed himself a handful of dirt. God looked at him and said, "No, No! You go get your own dirt!"

WHO STARTED CHRISTMAS?

This morning I heard a story on the radio of a woman who was out Christmas shopping with her two children. After many hours of looking at row after row of toys and everything else imaginable, and after hours of hearing both her children asking for everything they saw on those many shelves, she finally made it to the elevator with her two kids.

She was feeling what so many of us feel during the holiday season time of the year. Overwhelming pressure to go to every party, every housewarming, taste all the holiday food and treats, getting that perfect gift for every single person on our shopping list, making sure we don't forget anyone on our card list, and the pressure of making sure we respond to everyone who sent us a card.

Finally the elevator doors opened and there was already a crowd in the car. She pushed her way into the car and dragged her two kids in with her and all the bags of stuff. When the doors closed she couldn't take it anymore and stated, "Whoever started this whole Christmas thing should be found, strung up and shot."

From the back of the car everyone heard a quiet calm voice respond, "Don't worry we already crucified him."

For the rest of the trip down, the elevator it was so quiet you could have heard a pin drop.

My Note: Don't forget this year to keep the one who started this whole Christmas thing in your every thought, deed, purchase, and word, if we all did it, just think of how different this whole world would be.

DANIEL

    I sat, with two friends, in the picture window of a quaint restaurant just off the corner of the town square. The food and the company were both especially good that day.

    As we talked, my attention was drawn outside, across the street. There, walking into town was a man who appeared to be carrying all his worldly goods on his back. He was carrying, a well-worn sign that read, "I will work for food." My heart sank. I brought him to the attention of my friends and noticed that others around us had stopped eating to focus on him. Heads moved in a mixture of sadness and disbelief. We continued with our meal, but his image lingered in my mind. We finished our meal and went our separate ways. I had errands to do and quickly set out to accomplish them. I glanced toward the town square, looking somewhat halfheartedly for the strange visitor. I was fearful, knowing that seeing him again would call some response. I drove through town and saw nothing of him. I made some purchases at a store and got back in my car. Deep within me, the spirit of God kept speaking to me: "Don't go back to the office until you've at least driven once more around the square." And so, with some hesitancy, I headed back into town. As I turned the square's third corner. I saw him. He was standing on the steps of the storefront church, going through his sack. I stopped and looked; feeling both compelled to speak to him, yet wanting to drive on.

    The empty parking space on the corner seemed to be a sign from God: an invitation to park. I pulled in, got out and approached the town's newest visitor. "Looking for the pastor?" I asked. "Not really," he replied, "just resting." "Have you eaten today?" "Oh, I ate something early this morning." "Would you like to have lunch with me?" "Do you have some work I could do for you?" "No work," I replied. "I commute here to work from the city, but I would like to take you to lunch." "Sure," he replied with a smile. As he began to gather his things I asked some surface questions. "Where you headed?" "St Louis." "Where you from?" "Oh, all over, mostly Florida." "Fourteen years," came the reply. I knew I had met someone unusual. We sat across from each other in the same restaurant I had left earlier.

    His face was weathered slightly beyond his 38 years. His eyes were dark yet clear, and he spoke with an eloquence and articulation that was startling. He removed his jacket to reveal a bright red T-shirt that said, "Jesus is The Never Ending Story." Then Daniel's story began to unfold. He had seen rough times early in life. He'd made some wrong choices and reaped the consequences. Fourteen years earlier, while backpacking across the country, he had stopped on the beach in Daytona. He tried to hire on with some men who were putting up a large tent and some equipment. A concert, he thought. He was hired, but the tent would not house a concert but revival services, and in those services he saw life more clearly. He gave his life over to God. "Nothing's been the same since," he said, "I felt the Lord telling me to keep walking, and so I did, some 14 years now."

"Ever think of stopping?" I asked. "Oh, once in a while, when it seems to get the best of me. But God has given me this calling. I give out Bibles. That's what's in my sack. I work to buy food and Bibles, and I give them out when His Spirit leads."

I sat amazed. My homeless friend was not homeless. He was on a mission and lived this way by choice. The questions burned inside for a moment and then I asked; "What's it like?" "What?" "To walk into a town carrying all your things on your back and to show your sign?" "Oh, it was humiliating at first. People would stare and make comments. Once someone tossed a piece of half-eaten bread and made a gesture that certainly didn't make me feel welcome. But then it became humbling to realize that God was using me to touch lives and change people's concepts of other folks like me." My concept was changing, too. We finished our dessert and gathered his things. Just outside the door, he paused. He turned to me and said, "Come Ye blessed of my Father and inherit the kingdom I've prepared for you. For when I was hungry you gave me food, when I was thirsty you gave me drink, a stranger and you took me in." I felt as if we were on holy ground. "Could you use another Bible?" I asked. He said he preferred a certain translation. It traveled well and was not too heavy. It was also his personal favorite. "I've read through it 14 times," he said. "I'm not sure we've got one of those, but let's stop by our church and see." I was able to find my new friend a Bible that would do well, and he seemed very grateful.

"Where you headed from here?" "Well, I found this little map on the back of this amusement park coupon." "Are you hoping to hire on there for a while?" "No, I just figure I should go there. I figure someone under that star right there needs a Bible, so that's where I'm going next." He smiled, and the warmth of his spirit radiated the sincerity of his mission. I drove him back to the town-square where we'd met two hours earlier, and as we drove, it started raining. We parked and unloaded his things. "Would you sign my autograph book?" he asked. "I like to keep messages from folks I meet."

    I wrote in his little book that his commitment to his calling had touched my life. I encouraged him to stay strong. And I left him with a verse of scripture from Jeremiah, "I know the plans I have for you," declared the Lord, "plans to prosper you and not to harm you. Plans to give you a future and a hope." "Thanks, man," he said. "I know we just met and we're really just strangers, but I love you." "I know," I said, "I love you, too." "The Lord is good." "Yes, He is. How long has it been since someone hugged you?" I asked. "A long time," he replied.

And so on the busy street corner in the drizzling rain, my new friend and I embraced, and I felt deep inside that I had been changed. He put his things on his back, smiled his winning smile and said, "See you in the New Jerusalem." "I'll be there!" was my reply. He began his journey again. He headed away with his sign dangling from his bedroll and pack of Bibles. He stopped, turned and said, "When you see something that makes you think of me, will you pray for me?" "You bet," I shouted back, "God bless." "God bless." And that was the last I saw of him.

Late that evening as I left my office, the wind blew strong. The cold front had settled hard upon the town. I bundled up and hurried to my car. As I sat back and reached for the emergency brake, I saw them a pair of well-worn brown work gloves neatly laid over the length of the handle. I picked them up and thought of my friend and wondered if his hands would stay warm that night without them. I remembered his words: "If you see something that makes you think of me, will you pray for me?" Today his gloves lie on my desk in my office. They help me to see the world and its people in a new way, and they help me remember those two hours with my unique friend and to pray for his ministry. "See you in the New Jerusalem, he said. Yes, Daniel, I know I will.

<u>My Note</u>: You are all now my new friends. I share this story with you because, "I shall pass this way but once." Therefore, any good that I can do or any kindness that I can show let me do it now, for I shall not pass this way again". God Bless You All)

Humor Break: 　　　　　　　LIPSTICK

The junior high school principal had a problem with some girls who were starting to use lipstick. When applying it in the bathroom they would blot their lips on the mirrors, leaving lip prints. So he spoke to the teachers and asked for their help. They promised they would speak to the girls, but after two weeks, the situation didn't improve at all. He even called a few of the girls' parents who were his friends for their advice, but to no avail. The mirrors were constantly a mess.

Finally he thought of a way to stop it. One day he gathered together all the girls who wore lipstick. He then took them into the bathroom and lectured about how hard it was to clean the lipstick off the mirrors. You could see the young girls smiling at each other, all nodding publicly but smirking to one another. The principal then asked the custodian, who was present, to demonstrate how difficult it was to clean the mirrors. The custodian took a long handled brush, dipped it into the toilet and vigorously rubbed the lipstick off the mirrors. From that day forward, the mirrors stayed lipstick free.

TRAGEDY OR BLESSING?

Years ago in Scotland, the Clark Family had a dream. Clark and his wife worked and saved, making plans for their children and them to travel to the United States. It had taken years, but they had finally saved enough money and had gotten passports and reservations for the whole family on a new liner to the United States.

The entire family was filled with anticipation and excitement about their new life. However, seven days before their departure, a dog bit the youngest son. The doctor sewed up the boy but hung a yellow sheet on the Clarks front door. Because of the possibility of rabies, they were being quarantined for fourteen days. The family's dreams were dashed. They would not be able to make the trip to America as they had planned.

The father filled with disappointment and anger, stomped to the dock to watch the ship the ship leave without the Clark family. The father shed tears of disappointment and cursed both his son and God for their misfortune.

Five days later, the tragic news spread throughout Scotland, the mighty Titanic had sunk. The unsinkable ship had sunk, taking hundreds of lives with it. The Clark family was to have been on that ship, but because a dog had bitten the son, they were left behind in Scotland.

When Mr. Clark heard the news, he hugged his son and thanked him for saving the family.

He thanked God for saving their lives and turning what he had felt was a tragedy into a blessing.

My Note: Although we may not always understand, all things happen for a reason.

ALL THE TIME IN THE WORLD

While at the park one day, a woman sat down next to a man on a bench near a playground. "That's my son over there," she said, pointing to a little boy in a red sweater who was gliding down the slide. "He's a fine looking boy," the man said. "That's my son on the swing in the blue sweater." Then, looking at his watch, he called to his son. "What do you say we go, Todd?" Todd pleaded, "Just five more minutes, Dad please? Just five more minutes." The man nodded and Todd continued to swing to his hearts content. Minutes passed and the father stood and called again to his son. "Time to go now?" Again Todd pleaded. "Five more minutes. Please just five more minutes." The man smiled and said, "Okay." "My, you certainly are a patient father," the woman responded.

The man smiled and then said, "My older son Tommy was killed by a drunk driver last year while he was riding his bike near hear. I never spent much time with tommy and now I'd give anything for just five more minutes with him. I've vowed not to make the same mistake with Todd.

Besides, "He thinks he has five more minutes to swing. The truth is, I get five more minutes to watch him play."

<u>My Note</u>: My children are adults now and I would give anything to have them as children again.

GOT TO LOVE THIS JUDGE!!!

In Florida, an atheist became incensed over the preparation for Easter and Passover holidays and decided to contact the local ACLU about the discrimination inflicted on atheists by the constant celebrations afforded to Christians and Jews with all their holidays while the atheists had no holiday to celebrate.

The ACLU jumped on the opportunity to once again pick up the cause of the godless and assigned their sharpest attorney's to the case. The case was brought before a wise judge who after listening to the long, passionate presentation of the ACLU lawyers promptly banged his gavel and declared, "Case dismissed!"

The lead ACLU lawyer immediately stood and objected to the ruling and said, "Your honor, how can you possibly dismiss this case? Surely the Christians have Christmas, Easter and many other observances. And the Jews, why in addition to Passover they have Yom Kippur and Hanukkah, and yet my client and all other atheists have no such holiday!"

The judge leaned forward in his chair and simply said "Obviously your client is too confused to know about or for that matter even celebrate the atheists' holiday!" The ACLU lawyer pompously said "We are aware of no such holiday for atheists, just what might that be, your honor?"

The judge said "Well it comes every year on exactly the same date…April 1st" "The fool says in his heart, "There is no God." (Psalm 14:1) (Psalm 53:1)   **_MY Note_**: You just **_got_** to love this judge.

CHILDREN

If a child lives with Criticism, he learns to condemn.

If a child lives with hostility, he learns to fight.

If a child lives with fear, he learns to be apprehensive.

If a child lives with pity, he learns to feel sorry for himself.

If a child lives with ridicule, he learns to be shy.

If a child lives with jealousy, he learns to feel guilty.

If a child lives with tolerance, he learns to be patient.

If a child lives with encouragement, he learns to be confident.

If a child lives with praise, he learns to be appreciative.

If a child lives with acceptance, he learns to love.

If a child lives with approval, he learns to like himself.

If a child lives with honesty, he learns to be truthful.

If a child lives with fairness, he learns justice.

If a child lives with security, he learns to have faith in himself and others.

My Note: I have a question: What is your child living?

Humor Break: A CUP OF TEA

One day my mother was out, and my dad was in charge of me. I was maybe 2 ½ years old. Someone had given me a little "Tea Set" as a gift, and it was one of my toys.

Daddy was in the living room engrossed in the evening news when I brought him a little cup of "tea", which was just water. After several cups of tea and lots of praise for such yummy tea, my mom came home.

My dad made her wait in the living room to watch me bring him a cup of tea, because it was "just the cutest thing!" Mom waited, and sure enough, here I came down the hall with a cup of tea for Daddy; and she watched him drink it up.

Then she said, (as only a mother would know), "Did it ever occur to you that the only place she can reach to get water, is the toilet?"

INSPIRATIONAL SLOGANS

I want to leave you with a list of inspirational slogans, sayings, etc. These are things that I have heard, read, and even used in my career as a teacher and coach. I have also applied them to my everyday dealings with people and situations that I have encountered.

1. God is first, you are second, and I am third!
2. No Pain – No Gain.
3. If you are not out practicing – Someone is out practicing you!
4. Before you can score – You must first have a goal.
5. Discipline yourself so that others won't have to.
6. Teamwork means success – Work Together – Win Together.
7. What you practice, not what you preach is what you spread.
8. Triumph is just "Umph" added to try.
9. You aren't worth a nickel unless you make your grades.
10. Have patience, all things are difficult before they become easy.
11. Profanity never made a lady out of a girl.
12. No one has ever drowned in sweat.
13. The only place success comes before work is in the dictionary.
14. Things turn out for the best for those who make the best of the way things turn out.
15. Nothing is "Opened by mistake" more often than the mouth.
16. When you are through learning, you are through.
17. There is no "I" in team.
18. Be careful of how you spend your free time. If you lay down with Dogs you'll get up with fleas.

19. Choose your companions carefully, you are what they are.
20. If what you have done yesterday still looks big to you today, then you haven't done much today.
21. Success depends on backbone – not wishbone.
22. Getting together is a beginning, working together is progress, staying together is success.
23. Enthusiasm is contagious – are you spreading it?
24. American ends in "I can".
25. He/ She can who thinks He/ She can.
26. Attitudes are contagious – is yours worth catching?
27. When you quit trying to be better, you will never be good.
28. Once you know how to do it correctly – you can do it right the rest of your life.
29. Work will win – wishing won't.
30. You can't be a night owl and compete with the eagles during the day.
31. The good player keeps in training without being asked (or told)!
32. Profane language does not make a man out of a boy.
33. Profanity is an unintelligent way of expressing oneself.

Your last Humor Break: THE SHOE BOX

A man and woman had been married for more than 60 years. They had shared everything. They had talked about everything. They had kept no secrets from each other except that the little Old woman had a shoe box in the top of her closet that she had cautioned her husband never to open or ask her about.

For all of these years, he had never thought about the box, but one day the little old woman got very sick and the doctor said she would not recover.

In trying to sort out their affairs, the little old man took down the shoe box and took it to his wife's bedside. She agreed that it was time that he should know what was in the box. When he opened it, he found two crocheted dolls and a stack of money totaling $95,000 dollars.

He asked her about the contents. When we were to be married, my grandmother told me the secret of a happy marriage was to never argue. She told me that if I ever got angry with you, I should just keep quiet and crochet a doll.

The little old man was so moved; he had to fight back tears. Only two precious dolls were in the box. She had only been angry with him two times in all those years of living and loving... He almost burst with happiness.

Honey, he said, that explains the doll, but what about all of this money? Where did it come from?

Oh, she said, that's the money I made from selling the dolls.

Made in the USA
San Bernardino, CA
19 December 2013